WHAT IS FREEDOM?

How Does It Ring?

Angela Landon

AuthorHouse™
1663 Liberty Drive
Bloomington, IN 47403
www.authorhouse.com
Phone: 833-262-8899

This book is printed on acid-free paper.

ISBN: 978-1-4567-4538-7 (sc)
ISBN: 978-1-4772-0728-4 (e)

Library of Congress Control Number: 2011904614

Print information available on the last page.

Published by AuthorHouse 01/23/2024

authorHOUSE®

What is freedom?

How does it ring?

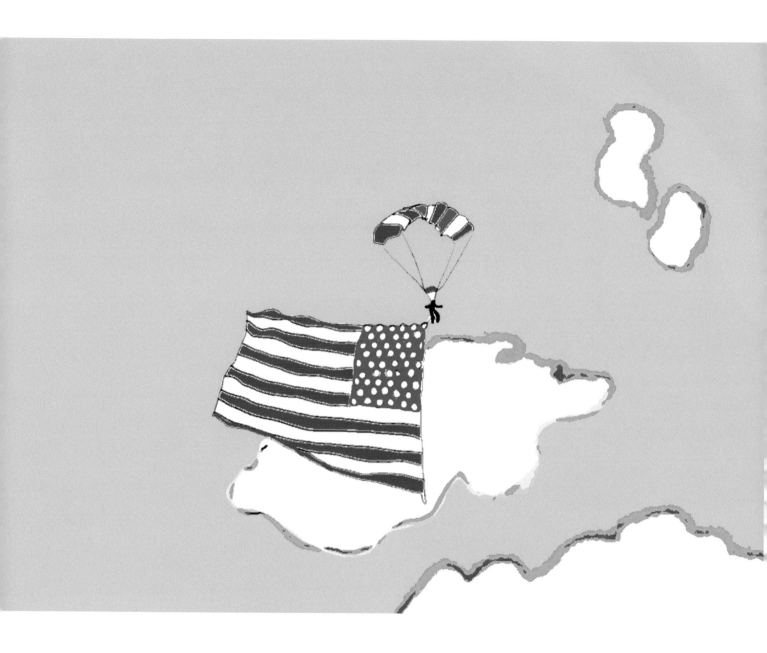

Is it something you hold?

Is it something you sing?

In America I am free,

to go to any school.

My parents can choose it.

I think that's cool.

It doesn't matter,

if I'm a girl or a boy,

We all can learn

and experience the joy.

We are free to worship our Lord and God,

in any church or synagogue.

My parents can vote. They have a choice.

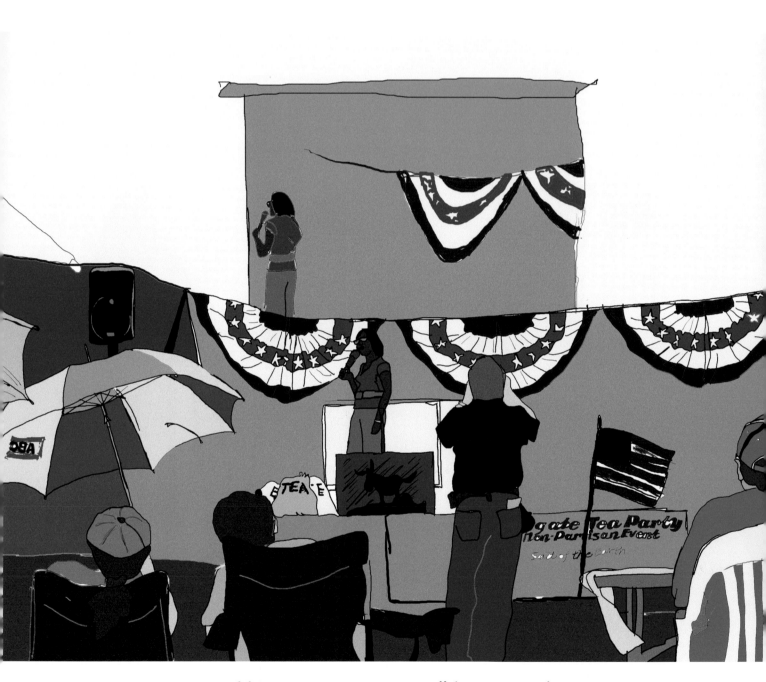

Man or woman, we all have a voice.

In America you can say what you think.

Shout it from the roof tops,

or print it in ink.

So when you say the pledge or salute the flag,

remember it's OK to brag.

Think of those who made us free,

from plain to shore,

from mountain to sea.

This freedom did not come without cost.

It is a gift from those who lost,

their lives so we might all be free,

free to be you,
free to be me.

This is freedom.

Do you hear it ring?

It rings in my heart!

It means a lot to me.

Say Thank You.
Find a soldier or a veteran to write to. It may be a neighbor, a family member or a friend. Ask at your school or church, or check the many websites online for help. Here is one. They would love to hear from you.
www.anysoldier.com

Notes

Printed in the United States
by Baker & Taylor Publisher Services